U.S.A. TRAVEL GUIDES

WYOMING

BY ANN HEINRICHS • ILLUSTRATED BY MATT KANIA

Published by The Child's World®
1980 Lookout Drive • Mankato, MN 56003-1705
800-599-READ • www.childsworld.com

Photo Credits

Photographs ©: Edwin Verin/Shutterstock Images,
cover, 1; Shutterstock Images, 7, 37 (top); 37 (bottom);
iStockphoto, 8, 16; Juan Monino/iStockphoto, 11;
Kobby Dagan/Shutterstock Images, 12, 31; Sue
Smith/Shutterstock Images, 15; Ben Krut/iStockphoto,
19; Barbagallo Franco/Hemis/Alamy, 20; Eugeniy
Chernetcov/iStockphoto, 23; Lincoln Rogers/Shutterstock
Images, 24; Phil Augustavo/iStockphoto, 27; Wit Gorski/
iStockphoto, 28; Philip Scalia/Alamy, 32; Jeffrey M.
Frank/Shutterstock Images, 35

ISBN 9781503819900
LCCN 2016961200

Printing

Printed in the United States of America
PA02334

Ann Heinrichs is the author
of more than 100 books
for children and young
adults. She has also enjoyed
successful careers as a
children's book editor and
an advertising copywriter.
Ann grew up in Fort Smith,
Arkansas, and lives in
Chicago, Illinois.

About the Author
Ann Heinrichs

Matt Kania loves maps and, as a
kid, dreamed of making them. In
school he studied geography and
cartography, and today he makes
maps for a living. Matt's favorite
thing about drawing maps is
learning about the places they
represent. Many of the maps
he has created can be found in
books, magazines, videos, Web
sites, and public places.

About the
Map Illustrator
Matt Kania

*On the cover: Devils Tower National
Monument is in northeastern Wyoming.*

OUR WYOMING TRIP

Y ou're in for a great trip through Wyoming! Just follow that dotted line. Or else skip around. Either way, you're in for lots of fun!

You'll hang out with cowboys and mountain men. You'll see where famous outlaws hid. You'll watch water spewing into the air. You'll pan for gold and stay on a ranch. And you'll dig for dinosaur bones!

There's plenty more to do in Wyoming. So buckle up and let's hit the road!

WELCOME TO
WYOMING

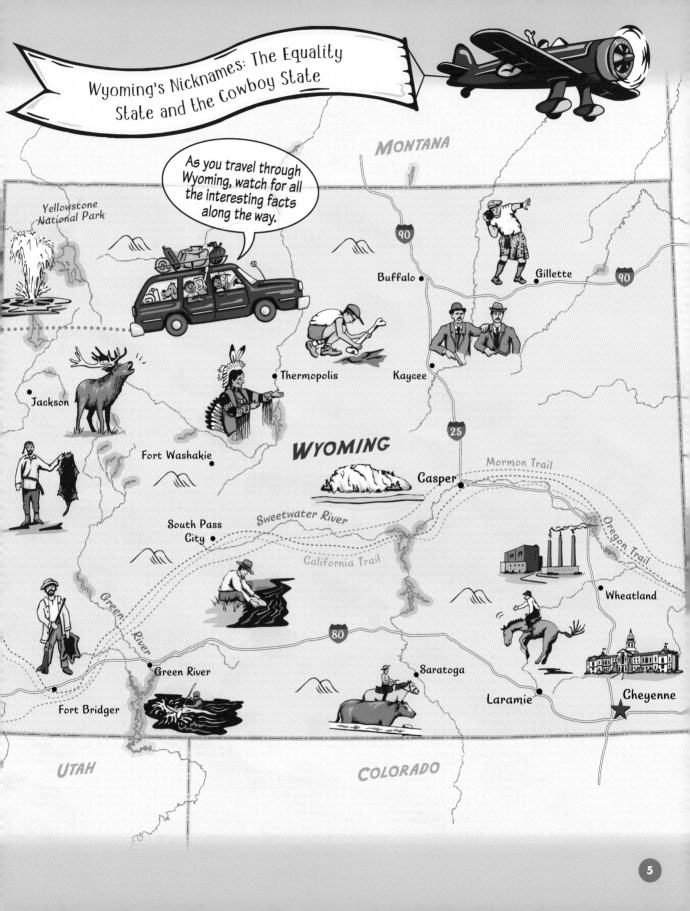

The Black Hills rise in northeastern Wyoming. They continue into South Dakota.

Old Faithful is Yellowstone's most famous geyser. It erupts every 45 to 90 minutes.

MONTANA

Yellowstone National Park

Cody •

• Basin

Crook County

Black Hills

Pew! Why are these mud pots so stinky? Because hydrogen sulfide is coming out. That's also known as "rotten egg gas"!

Belle Fourche River

Teton Range

• Moran

Rocky Mountains

• Thermopolis
Wind River Canyon

Jackson

Gannett Peak

Diversion Dam

Green River

Highest Temperature: Basin August 8, 1983 Diversion Dam August 15, 1988 115°F (46°C)

Lowest Temperature: Moran February 9, 1933 –66°F (–54°C)

HIGHEST AND LOWEST POINTS
HIGHEST: Gannett Peak at 13,804 feet (4,207 m)
LOWEST: Belle Fourche River in Crook County at 3,100 feet (945 m)

Wind River Canyon is south of Thermopolis. It has many scenic rock formations. The canyon is a good place to study geology.

Yellowstone's main entrances in Wyoming are Jackson and Cody.

COLORADO

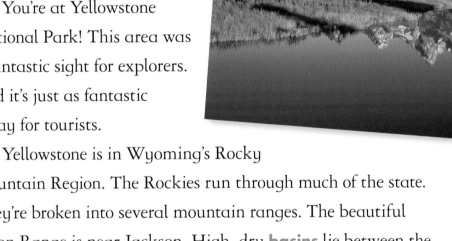

Bubbling **mud pots** are belching out gases. **Geysers** are spewing super-hot water high into the air. You're at Yellowstone National Park! This area was a fantastic sight for explorers. And it's just as fantastic today for tourists.

Yellowstone is in Wyoming's Rocky Mountain Region. The Rockies run through much of the state. They're broken into several mountain ranges. The beautiful Teton Range is near Jackson. High, dry **basins** lie between the mountain ranges.

High plains cover eastern Wyoming. Thousands of cattle and sheep graze there. Some rivers have carved out deep canyons. One such river is the Green River. It flows through western Wyoming.

The peaks of the Teton Range are nearly 7,000 feet (2,134 m) tall.

THE NATIONAL ELK REFUGE

Thousands of elk move across the snowy ground. They look like big, shaggy deer. You're visiting the National Elk Refuge! It's north of Jackson. More than 7,500 elk spend the winter here.

Elk are some of Wyoming's largest animals. Grizzly bears and moose are big ones, too. You'll see mountain sheep high in the Rockies. Mountain lions also lurk in the mountains. Deer and antelope graze on the plains.

Wyoming also has lots of smaller animals. There are beavers, raccoons, ferrets, foxes, and rabbits. Trappers used to hunt some of them. Then they sold the furry skins.

Dusk and dawn are the best times to see elk.

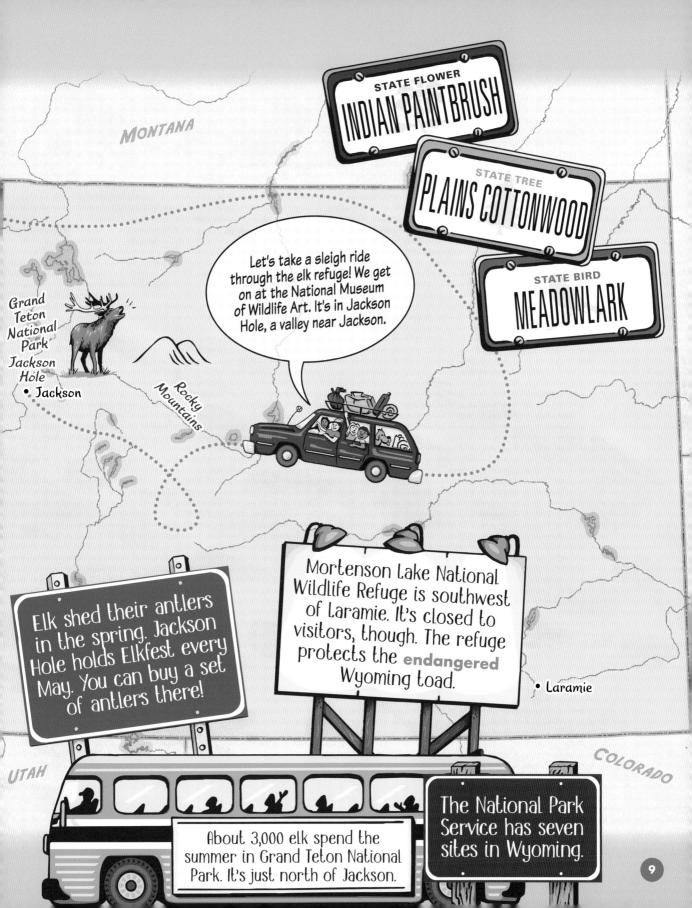

STATE FLOWER
INDIAN PAINTBRUSH

STATE TREE
PLAINS COTTONWOOD

STATE BIRD
MEADOWLARK

MONTANA

Let's take a sleigh ride through the elk refuge! We get on at the National Museum of Wildlife Art. It's in Jackson Hole, a valley near Jackson.

Grand Teton National Park
Jackson Hole
• Jackson

Rocky Mountains

Elk shed their antlers in the spring. Jackson Hole holds Elkfest every May. You can buy a set of antlers there!

Mortenson Lake National Wildlife Refuge is southwest of Laramie. It's closed to visitors, though. The refuge protects the endangered Wyoming toad.

• Laramie

UTAH

COLORADO

About 3,000 elk spend the summer in Grand Teton National Park. It's just north of Jackson.

The National Park Service has seven sites in Wyoming.

EASTERN SHOSHONE INDIAN DAYS

Want to learn about Native American **cultures**? Then attend Eastern Shoshone Indian Days in Fort Washakie. It's on the Wind River Indian **Reservation**.

Powwows are celebrations of Native American cultures. At powwows, Native American people can celebrate the history and heritage of their particular Native American nation. People come from far away to take part. They wear **traditional** dress. And they compete in dancing and drumming contests.

Many Native American groups once lived in Wyoming, such as the Arapaho, Bannock, Cheyenne, Kiowa, Nez Percé, Sioux, and Shoshone. However, these Native Americans were forced off their land by the U.S. government. Today, there are only two major tribes in Wyoming. They are the Arapaho and Shoshone Tribes.

Beautiful traditional outfits are worn at the Eastern Shoshone Indian Days celebration.

Watch the bow-and-arrow contest. See how mountain men started campfires without matches. Or check out the kids' games. Native American drummers and dancers are performing. And tents and tepees surround the camp. It's Fort Bridger's Mountain Man **Rendezvous**! This event is held each year in early September.

Wyoming was once part of France's Louisiana Territory. The United States bought this region in 1803. Then explorers and fur trappers came into Wyoming. Fur trappers met at a rendezvous every summer. They told stories and played games. It was a great party!

Watch the blacksmith demonstration at the Mountain Man Rendezvous.

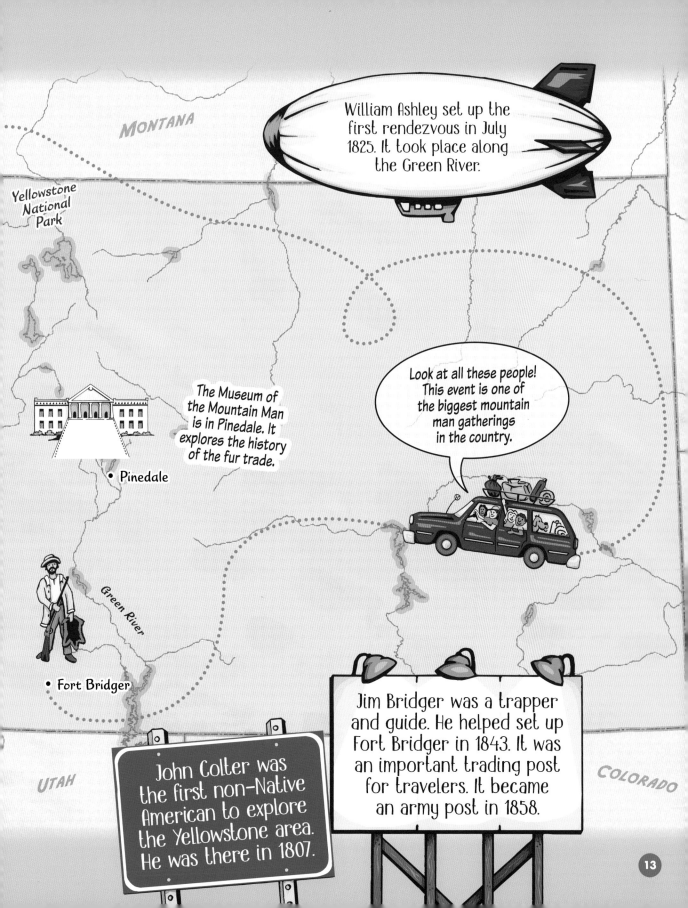

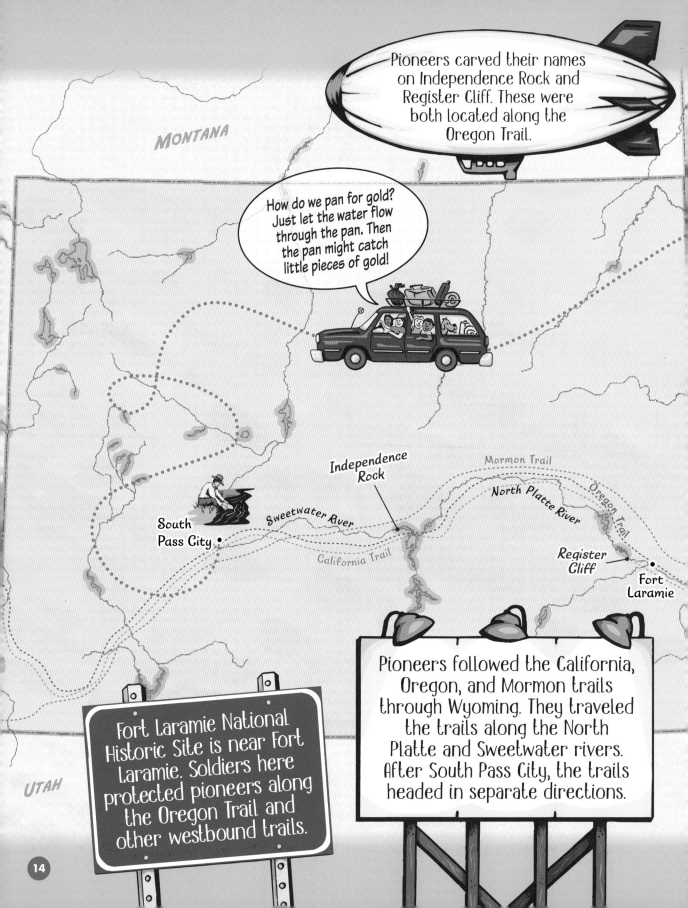

GOLD RUSH DAYS IN SOUTH PASS CITY

Are you ready to pan for gold in the creek near South Pass City? It's time for Gold Rush Days! It's at South Pass City State Historic Site.

Many pioneers began heading west in the 1840s. Their trails went through South Pass. It was a well-known passage through the mountains.

Gold was discovered in Wyoming in 1867. It was in the mountains west of South Pass. Thousands of eager gold miners swarmed into town. Gold lured miners through northern and eastern Wyoming, too.

Old buildings are preserved in historic South Pass City.

OVERLAND STAGE STAMPEDE RODEO

Speak with cowboys and cowgirls. Watch them ride a bucking bull. You're at the Overland Stage Stampede Rodeo! It's held in Green River. This event takes place at the beginning of June each year.

Lots of people pass through the town of Green River. They're heading into Flaming Gorge National Recreation Area. This deep canyon has colorful rock walls. The Green River runs through it.

John Wesley Powell explored this river in 1869. He began his journey in the town of Green River. It was called Green River City then. He followed the Green River to where it meets the Colorado River in Utah. Then he continued on the Colorado River through Arizona's Grand Canyon.

Rodeos are a popular event in Wyoming!

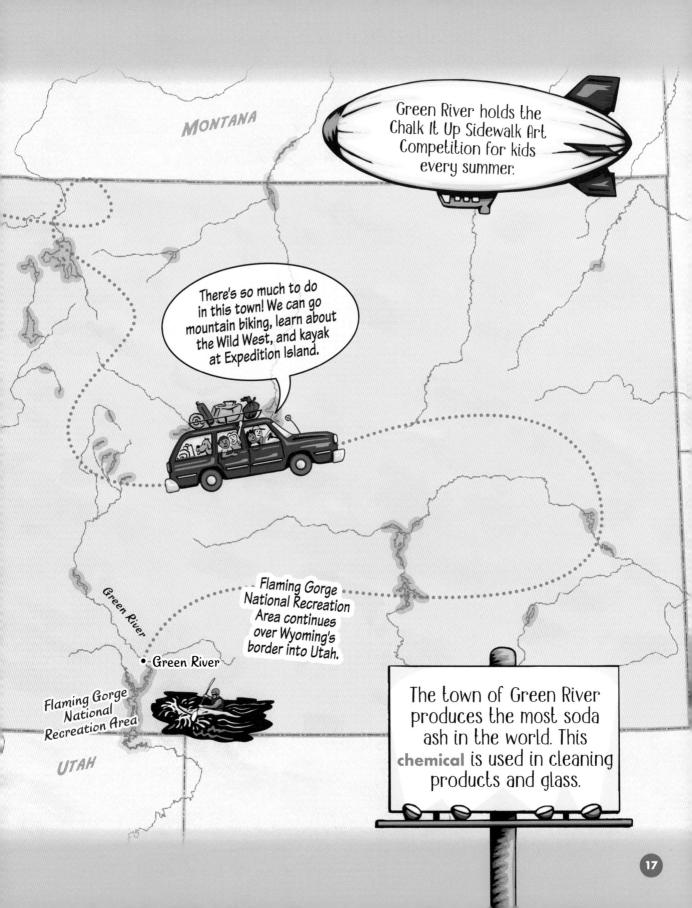

Wyoming's state motto is "Equal Rights."

MONTANA

Esther Hobart Morris worked hard for women's rights. Morris died in Cheyenne in 1902.

Wyoming women first served on a jury in Laramie in 1870.

South Pass City

WYOMING WAS THE
FIRST STATE TO . . .
Let women vote
Let women serve on juries
Let women legally own property
Let women hold public offices

• Laramie

★ Cheyenne

COLORA

Nellie Tayloe Ross was Wyoming's first female governor. She was elected in 1924. Ross was director of the U.S. Mint from 1933 to 1953.

Wyoming is called the Equality State because it granted women equal rights long before other states did.

UTAH

THE STATE CAPITOL IN CHEYENNE

See that statue in front of the capitol? It's Esther Hobart Morris. She made history in 1870. She became South Pass City's justice of the peace. That's a type of judge. Morris served for about eight months. No woman had ever held such a post before. The statue stands as a symbol of women's rights.

The capitol is Wyoming's state government building in Cheyenne. The state government is divided into three branches. One branch makes state laws. Its members meet in the capitol. Another branch sees that laws are obeyed. The governor heads this branch. Judges make up the third branch. They decide whether laws have been broken.

The cornerstone for the capitol building was laid in 1887.

OUTLAWS AND CATTLE WARS

Can you name some famous outlaws? How about Butch Cassidy and the Sundance Kid? They were bank robbers and horse thieves. They had a hideout in Wyoming. It was called Hole-in-the-Wall!

Hole-in-the-Wall is a rocky canyon full of caves. You can visit this spot near Kaycee. You can even stay at nearby guest ranches. One is the famous TA Ranch in Buffalo.

Some ranchers believed people were stealing their cattle. They decided to take the law into their own hands. They formed a group called the Invaders. Their purpose? To find the thieves! This was called the Johnson County War. The Invaders were finally captured at the TA Ranch.

A trail leads to the top of the red rocks near Hole-in-the-Wall.

Wyoming passed laws in 1886 that created free county libraries.

MONTANA

Let's stay at the TA Ranch! We can ride horses and help the cowboys round up cattle!

Sundance •

• Buffalo

Ten Sleep •

Johnson County

• Kaycee

The Johnson County War took place in 1892.

Harry Longabaugh was jailed in Sundance for stealing a horse, gun, and saddle. That's how he got his nickname— the Sundance Kid!

Wyoming was the 44th state to enter the Union. It joined on July 10, 1890.

COLORADO

Cattle and sheep ranchers fought over grazing land. This led to the murder of three sheep ranchers near Ten Sleep in 1909.

Butch Cassidy's real name was Robert Leroy Parker. He stole cattle and horses.

DUDE RANCHING IN SARATOGA

Learn to care for a horse. Have a breakfast cookout around the campfire. Learn rope tricks from real cowboys. You're enjoying kids' programs at Brush Creek Ranch in Saratoga!

This is one of Wyoming's many dude ranches. *Dude* has a special meaning in the West. It's a city person unfamiliar with cowboy life.

Cattle ranching is Wyoming's biggest farm activity. Beef cattle are the most valuable farm products. Sheep and dairy cattle are important, too.

Most of Wyoming's farmland is naturally dry. But farmers use **irrigation** in their fields. Many farmers raise crops used as animal feed.

Ranching is hard work! Could you do it?

CHEYENNE FRONTIER DAYS

Watch the cowboys and cowgirls. Some are roping bulls. Some are racing around barrels on fast horses. And some are riding bucking **broncos**. You're in Cheyenne for Frontier Days! It has one of the world's largest rodeos.

Rodeos are popular events in Wyoming. And no wonder. Real cowboys work on all those ranches!

Millions of visitors come to Wyoming every year. Many visit Yellowstone and Grand Teton national parks. They hike through the wilderness or watch animals. The mountains are great for climbing and snowmobiling, too. In winter, skiers head for the snowy slopes. Jackson Hole near Jackson is a favorite skiing spot.

The stands are always full at the Frontier Days rodeo.

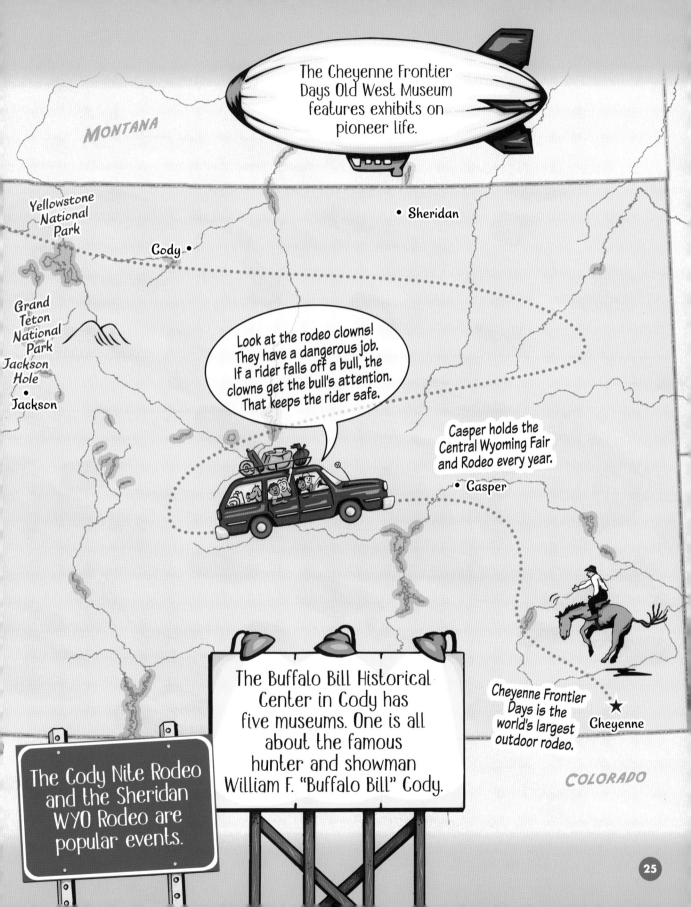

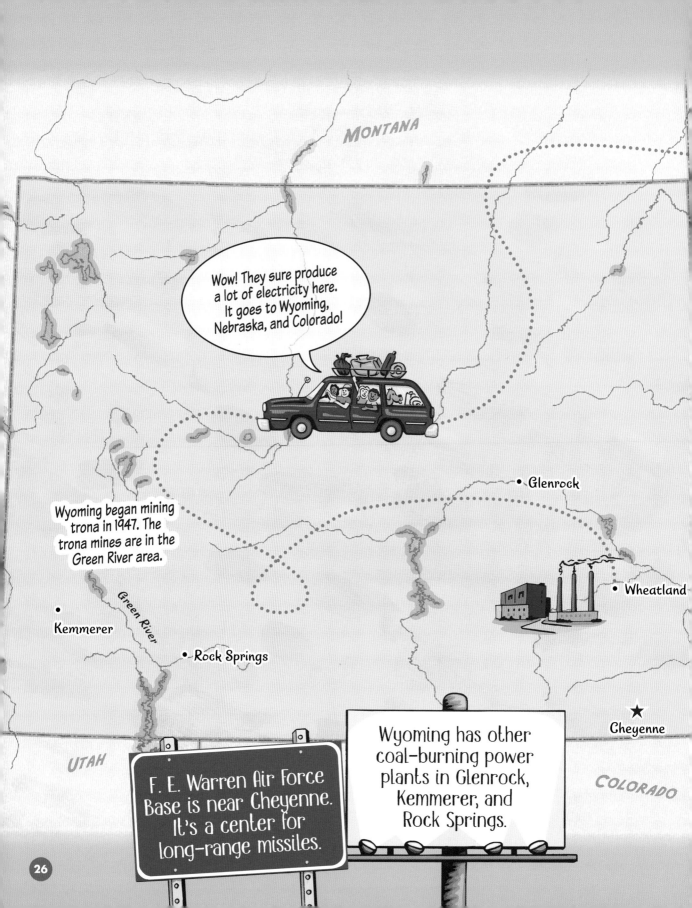

LARAMIE RIVER STATION

Tall smokestacks rise above the plains. You've reached the Laramie River Station! It's a big power plant near Wheatland. It burns coal to produce electricity. Step inside for a tour. You'll see its massive machines at work.

Wyoming has huge coal deposits. Many coal-burning power plants were built in the 1960s. Power plants can harm the **environment**. But workers at the Laramie River Station are careful. Equipment there helps protect the land, air, and water.

Wyoming produces more coal than any other state. It's rich in other minerals, too. One is trona. That's used in making glass, detergent, and paper. Another is bentonite. It's used to make paint, cosmetics, and crayons.

Wyoming supplies approximately 42 percent of the United States' coal.

27

JOURNEY THOUGH JACKSON

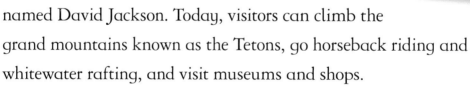

Mountains tower over the town of Jackson. Visitors fill the sidewalks as they walk from store to store. Others lace up their hiking shoes. There's lots to do in this town!

Jackson was named in 1894 after a mountain man named David Jackson. Today, visitors can climb the grand mountains known as the Tetons, go horseback riding and whitewater rafting, and visit museums and shops.

Jackson has a rich history. Fur traders used to pass through this area in the 1800s. Cattle ranching became a large business. Today, Wyoming has other well-known businesses. Chemicals are the leading factory goods. Soda ash is the major chemical product. It's made from the mineral trona. Many factories process oil, too. They take impure materials out of the oil. The oil can then be used to make gasoline.

In the winter, people can ski on the mountains in Jackson.

29

I want to try on a kilt! Those are traditional Scottish plaid skirts.

In 2016, 585,501 people lived in Wyoming. It's the smallest state by population.

Rock Springs holds International Day every year. It celebrates the food, clothing, music, and dancing of more than 50 nationalities.

POPULATION OF LARGEST CITIES

Cheyenne......................63,335
Casper..........................60,285
Gillette...........................32,649

CHEYENNE CELTIC FESTIVAL

Come to the Cheyenne Celtic Festival. People celebrate Scottish and Irish traditions here. You might see activities you've never heard of before!

Stop by and watch dance performances. Or listen to the bagpipes. When you get hungry, try some of the food. Much of it is made from Irish and Scottish recipes!

Many **immigrants** moved into Wyoming in the 1900s. German people were the largest immigrant group at that time. Others came from Norway and Sweden. Wyoming never got very crowded, though. It has the smallest population among all the states!

Bagpipes are a traditional Scottish instrument.

DIGGING FOR DINOS IN THERMOPOLIS

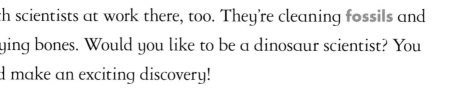

Want to go digging for dinosaurs? Just drop by the Wyoming Dinosaur Center in Thermopolis. It holds dino digs for kids and families. Real dinosaur scientists show you what to do.

Dinosaurs used to roam around here. Their remains are buried all over this area. Who knows? Maybe you'll find some bones!

Wander through the Dinosaur Center. It has life-size dinosaur models. You'll be amazed at how big these creatures were! You can watch scientists at work there, too. They're cleaning **fossils** and studying bones. Would you like to be a dinosaur scientist? You could make an exciting discovery!

The Wyoming Dinosaur Center has more than 30 dinosaur skeletons on display.

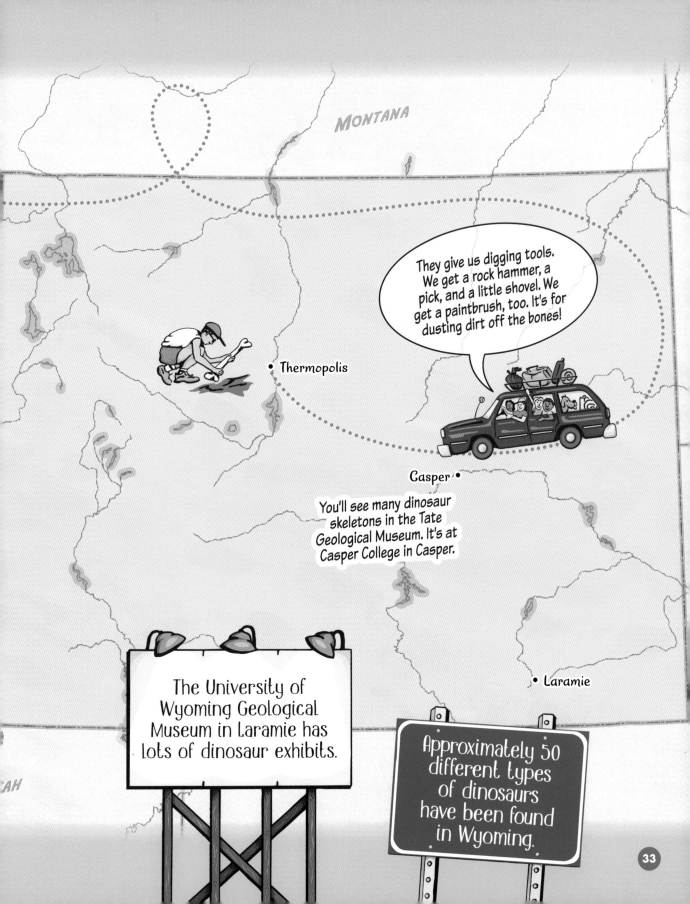

MONTANA

They give us digging tools. We get a rock hammer, a pick, and a little shovel. We get a paintbrush, too. It's for dusting dirt off the bones!

• Thermopolis

Casper •

You'll see many dinosaur skeletons in the Tate Geological Museum. It's at Casper College in Casper.

• Laramie

The University of Wyoming Geological Museum in Laramie has lots of dinosaur exhibits.

Approximately 50 different types of dinosaurs have been found in Wyoming.

UTAH

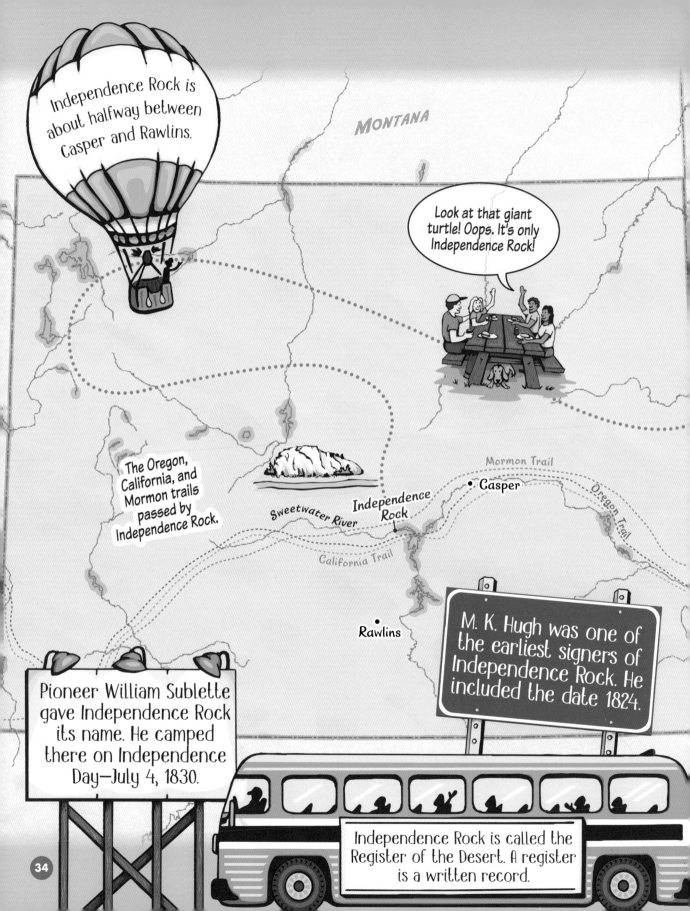

INDEPENDENCE ROCK

Pioneers knew Independence Rock well. It's right by the Sweetwater River. They could see the rock from far away. Some said it looked like an upside-down bowl. Others said it was like a giant turtle or whale.

Independence Rock was actually like a big bulletin board. Pioneers carved or painted their names on it. Some carved messages for friends who were coming later. It was exciting to find a friend's note!

Want to climb to the top of the rock? You'll see hundreds of names up there. It's fun to read the messages!

Independence Rock is 130 feet (40 m) high.

OUR TRIP

We visited many amazing places on our trip! We also met a lot of interesting people along the way. Look at the map below. Use your finger to trace all the places we have been.

How often does Old Faithful erupt? *See page 6 for the answer.*

When do elk shed their antlers? *Page 9 has the answer.*

What are stick games? *See page 10 for the answer.*

What trails did pioneers follow through Wyoming? *Look on page 14 for the answer.*

Where is the Chalk It Up Sidewalk Art Competition held? *See page 17 for the answer.*

Why is Wyoming called the Equality State? *Turn to page 18 for the answer.*

When did Wyoming begin mining trona? *See page 26 for the answer.*

How many types of dinosaurs have been found in Wyoming? *Page 33 has the answer.*

MONTANA

IDAHO

Yellowstone National Park

90

Buffalo

Gillette

90

SOUTH DAKOTA

Jackson

Thermopolis

Kaycee

Fort Washakie

WYOMING

25

Casper

Mormon Trail

NEBRASKA

South Pass City

Sweetwater River

California Trail

Oregon Trail

Green River

80

Wheatland

Fort Bridger

Green River

Saratoga

Laramie

Cheyenne

UTAH

COLORADO

STATE SYMBOLS

State bird: Western meadowlark

State dinosaur: *Triceratops*

State fish: Cutthroat trout

State flower: Indian paintbrush

State fossil: Knightia

State gemstone: Jade

State mammal: American bison (buffalo)

State reptile: Horned toad

State sport: Rodeo

State tree: Plains cottonwood

State flag

STATE SONG

"WYOMING"
Words by C. E. Winter, music by G. E. Knapp

In the far and mighty West,
Where the crimson sun seeks rest,
There's a growing splendid State
   that lies above,
On the breast of this great land;
Where the massive Rockies
   stand,
There's Wyoming young and
   strong, the State I love!

Chorus:
Wyoming, Wyoming! Land of the
   sunlight clear!
Wyoming, Wyoming! Land that
   we hold so dear!
Wyoming, Wyoming! Precious
   art thou and thine!
Wyoming, Wyoming! Beloved
   State of mine!

In the flowers wild and sweet,
Colors rare and perfumes meet;
There's the columbine so pure, the
   daisy too,
Wild the rose and red it springs,
White the button and its rings,
Thou art loyal for they're red and
   white and blue.

(Chorus)

Where thy peaks with crowned
   head,

Rising till the sky they wed,
Sit like snow queens ruling wood
   and stream and plain;
'Neath thy granite bases deep,
'Neath thy bosom's broadened
   sweep,
Lie the riches that have gained
   and brought thee fame.

(Chorus)

Other treasures thou dost hold,
Men and women thou dost
   mould,
True and earnest are the lives that
   thou dost raise,
Strengthen thy children thou dost
   teach,
Nature's truth thou givest to each,
Free and noble are thy workings
   and thy ways.

(Chorus)

In the nation's banner free
There's one star that has for me
A radiance pure and splendor
   like the sun;
Mine it is, Wyoming's star,
Home it leads me near or far;
O Wyoming! All my heart and
   love you've won!

That was a great trip! We have traveled all over Wyoming! There are a few places that we didn't have time for, though. Next time, we plan to visit the Ames Pyramid in Laramie. The pyramid was built to honor the Ames brothers. They manufactured shovels in the 1800s. Their shovels were used to dig for gold in California.

State seal

FAMOUS PEOPLE

Bridger, James (1804–1881), pioneer and mountain man

Buck, John (1980–), baseball player

Cheney, Dick (1941–), former vice president under President George W. Bush

Cody, William "Buffalo Bill" (1846–1917), scout and showman

Colter, John (ca. 1775–1813), explorer

Crazy Horse (ca. 1842–1877), Lakota Sioux Native American warrior

Dowler, Boyd (1937–), football player

Gardner, Rulon (1971–), athlete and Olympic medalist

Jackson, Harry (1924–2011), artist

MacLachlan, Patricia (1938–), children's author

Morris, Esther Hobart (1814–1902), women's rights pioneer

Rice, Travis (1982–), professional snowboarder

Ross, Nellie Tayloe (1876–1977), first woman governor in the United States

Smith, Jedediah (1799–1831), fur trader and explorer

Swallow, Alan (1915–1966), author and publisher

Washakie (ca. 1798–1900), Shoshone Native American leader

Yennie, Ashlynn (1985–), actress

WORDS TO KNOW

basins (BAY-sins) natural depressions on the earth's surface

broncos (BRAWN-koz) wild or partly tamed horses or ponies

chemical (KEM-uh-kuhl) a substance made by processing minerals in various ways

cultures (KUL-churz) the customs, beliefs, and ways of life of different groups of people

endangered (in-DAYN-jurd) in danger of dying off

environment (en-VYE-run-muhnt) natural surroundings, such as air, water, and soil

fossils (FOSS-uhlz) remains or prints of animals or plants left in stone

geology (jee-OL-uh-jee) the study of rocks

geysers (GUY-zurz) underground springs that spray out hot water and steam

immigrants (IM-uh-gruhnts) people who move to another country

irrigation (ihr-uh-GAY-shuhn) a method of bringing water to fields through ditches or pipes

mud pots (MUD pots) boiling pools of acid, clay, and hot water

rendezvous (RON-day-voo) a French word that means "meeting"

reservation (rez-ur-VAY-shuhn) land set aside for use by Native Americans

traditional (truh-DISH-uh-nul) following long-held customs

TO LEARN MORE

IN THE LIBRARY

Felix, Rebecca. *What's Great About Wyoming?* Minneapolis, MN: Lerner, 2016.

Hanson-Harding, Alexandra. *Wyoming.* New York, NY: Children's Press, 2009.

National Geographic Kids. *National Guide U.S.A.: The Most Amazing Sights, Scenes, and Cool Activities from Coast to Coast!* Washington, DC: National Geographic Society, 2012.

ON THE WEB

Visit our Web site for links about Wyoming:
childsworld.com/links

Note to Parents, Teachers, and Librarians: We routinely verify our Web links to make sure they are safe and active sites. So encourage your readers to check them out!

PLACES TO VISIT OR CONTACT

Travel Wyoming

travelwyoming.com
5611 High Plains Road
Cheyenne, WY 82007
307/777-7777
For more information about traveling in Wyoming

Wyoming State Museum

wyomuseum.state.wy.us
2301 Central Avenue
Cheyenne, WY 82002
307/777-7022
For more information about the history of Wyoming

Wyoming covers 97,813 square miles (253,335 sq km). It's the 10th-largest state in size.

INDEX

Bye, Equality State. We had a great time. We'll come back soon!